Master Maths at Home

Numbers to 10 Million

Scan the QR code to help your child's learning at home.

DK | MATHS NO PROBLEM!

mastermathsathome.com

How to use this book

Maths — No Problem! created **Master Maths at Home** to help children develop fluency in the subject and a rich understanding of core concepts.

Key features of the Master Maths at Home books include:

- Carefully designed lessons that provide structure, but also allow flexibility in how they're used.

- Speech bubbles containing content designed to spark diverse conversations, with many discussion points that don't have obvious 'right' or 'wrong' answers.

- Rich illustrations that will guide children to a discussion of shapes and units of measurement, allowing them to make connections to the wider world around them.

- Exercises that allow a flexible approach and can be adapted to suit any child's cognitive or functional ability.

- Clearly laid-out pages that encourage children to practise a range of higher-order skills.

- A community of friendly and relatable characters who introduce each lesson and come along as your child progresses through the series.

You can see more guidance on how to use these books at **mastermathsathome.com**.

We're excited to share all the ways you can learn maths!

Copyright © 2022 Maths — No Problem!

Maths — No Problem!
mastermathsathome.com
www.mathsnoproblem.com
hello@mathsnoproblem.com

First published in Great Britain in 2022 by
Dorling Kindersley Limited
One Embassy Gardens, 8 Viaduct Gardens, London SW11 7BW
A Penguin Random House Company

The authorised representative in the EEA is Dorling Kindersley
Verlag GmbH. Arnulfstr. 124, 80636 Munich, Germany

10 9 8 7 6 5 4 3 2 1
001–327105–May/22

A CIP catalogue record for this book is available from the British Library.

ISBN: 978-0-24153-949-1
Printed and bound in the UK

For the curious
www.dk.com

This book was made with Forest Stewardship Council™ certified paper - one small step in DK's commitment to a sustainable future. For more information go to www.dk.com/our-green-pledge

Acknowledgements
The publisher would like to thank the authors and consultants Andy Psarianos, Judy Hornigold, Adam Gifford and Dr Anne Hermanson.

The Castledown typeface has been used with permission from the Colophon Foundry.

Contents

Ruby   Elliott   Amira   Charles   Lulu   Sam   Oak   Holly   Ravi   Emma   Jacob   Hannah

Reading and writing numbers to 10 000 000 (part 1)

Starter

The population of Austria in 2020 was 8 917 205. How many millions of people is that?

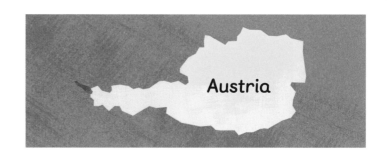

Austria

Example

We can show 8 917 205 using

1000000 100000 10000 1000 100 10 1 .

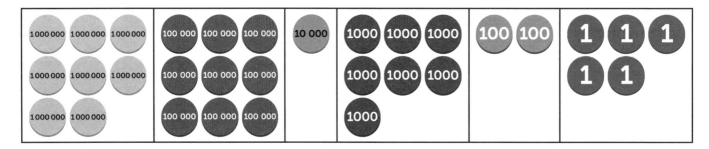

The 8 in 8 917 205 has a value of 8 000 000. It is in the millions place.

We read 8 000 000 as 8 million.

The 9 in 8 917 205 has a value of 900 000. It is in the hundred-thousands place.

The 1 in 8 917 205 has a value of 10 000. It is in the ten-thousands place.

The 7 in 8 917 205 has a value of 7000. It is in the thousands place.

The 2 in 8 917 205 has a value of 200. It is in the hundreds place.

The 0 in 8 917 205 has a value of 0. It is in the tens place.

The 5 in 8 917 205 has a value of 5. It is in the ones place.

We read 8 917 205 as eight million, nine hundred and seventeen thousand, two hundred and five.

There are no tens in 8 917 205.

1 Write the following numbers in numerals.

(a)

| 1 000 000 | 1 000 000 | 1 000 000 | 100 000 | 100 000 | 100 000 | 10 000 | 10 000 |
| 1 000 000 | 1 000 000 | | 100 000 | 100 000 | 100 000 | | |

five million, six hundred and twenty thousand

(b)

| 1 000 000 | 1 000 000 | 100 000 | 10 000 | 10 000 | 10 000 | 1000 | 1000 | 100 | 10 | 1 |

two million, one hundred and thirty-two thousand, one hundred and eleven

2 Write the following numbers in words.

(a) 2 456 000

(b) 6 125 230

(c) 8 912 652

Reading and writing numbers to 10 000 000 (part 2)

Starter

In 2020, Finland had 6 926 137 registered vehicles. Are there other ways to show 6 926 137?

Example

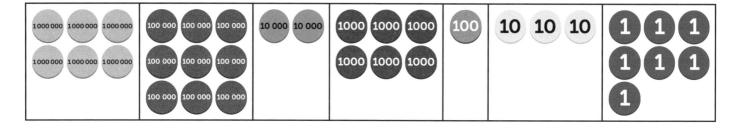

We read 6 926 137 as six million, nine hundred and twenty-six thousand, one hundred and thirty-seven.

We can break 6 926 137 into smaller values.

6 926 137 = 6 millions + 9 hundred thousands + 2 ten thousands + 6 thousands + 1 hundred + 3 tens + 7 ones

6 926 137 = 6 000 000 + 900 000 + 20 000 + 6000 + 100 + 30 + 7

The digit 6 is used twice in 6 926 137. Each 6 has a different value.

6 926 137

The 6 is in the millions place. Its value is 6 000 000.

The 6 is in the thousands place. Its value is 6000.

6000 is 1000 times smaller than 6 000 000.

6 000 000 is 1000 times greater than 6000.

Practice

1 Fill in the blanks.

(a) 4 532 128 = 4 000 000 + ⬚ + 30 000 + 2000 + ⬚
+ 20 + 8

(b) 7 659 382 = ⬚ + 600 000 + 50 000 + ⬚ +
⬚ + 80 + 2

(c) 2 413 926 = ⬚ + ⬚ + ⬚ +
⬚ + ⬚ + ⬚ + ⬚

2 Fill in the blanks to complete the sentences.

(a) 1000 is ⬚ times greater than 1.

(b) 30 000 is ⬚ times greater than 3000.

(c) 4000 is ⬚ times smaller than 400 000.

(d) 8000 is ⬚ times smaller than 8 000 000.

Comparing numbers to 10 000 000

Starter

Elliott put the populations of some countries into a table. How can he compare the populations?
What can Elliott say about this information?

Country	Population
Bulgaria	6 927 290
Costa Rica	5 094 110
Denmark	5 831 400
Finland	5 530 720
New Zealand	5 084 300
Norway	5 379 480
Singapore	5 685 810

Example

Each place value scales up or down by 10.

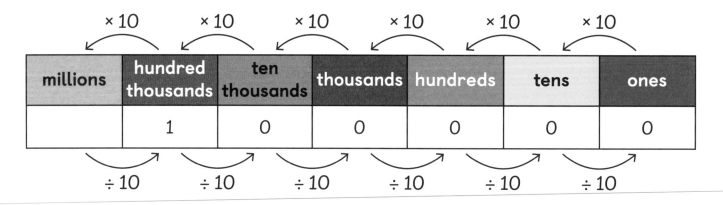

			× 10			
millions	hundred thousands	ten thousands	thousands	hundreds	tens	ones
	1	0	0	0	0	0

÷ 10

100 000 is 10 times greater than 10 000 and 10 times smaller than 1 000 000.

Compare the populations of Bulgaria and Singapore.

Bulgaria	6 927 290
Singapore	5 685 810

We do not need to look beyond the millions place.

6 millions will always be greater than 5 millions.

6 927 290 > 5 685 810

Bulgaria has a greater population than Singapore.

Compare the populations of Denmark and Finland.

Denmark	5 831 400
Finland	5 530 720

There are an equal number of millions.

We need to look at the digits in the next place.

8 hundred thousands are greater than 5 hundred thousands. We do not need to look beyond the hundred-thousands place.

5 831 400 > 5 530 720

Denmark has a greater population than Finland.

Compare the populations of New Zealand and Costa Rica.

New Zealand	5 084 300
Costa Rica	5 094 110

There are an equal number of millions. There are no hundred thousands.

There is 1 more ten thousand in 5 094 110 than in 5 084 300.

We do not need to look beyond the ten-thousands place to find the greater number.

5 084 300 < 5 094 110

New Zealand has a smaller population than Costa Rica.

Compare the populations of Norway and Denmark.

Norway	5 379 480
Denmark	5 831 400

Which place value tells us which country has the greater population?

The number of millions is equal. The number of hundred thousands is different.

We can tell which country has the greater population just by looking at the millions and hundred-thousands places.

5 379 480 < 5 831 400

Norway has a smaller population than Denmark.

Practice

1 Compare using > or <.

(a)

(b)

(c)

(d)

2 Compare using **greater than** or **less than**.

(a) 6 800 000 is [ ] than 5 800 000.

(b) 4 030 000 is [ ] than 4 003 000.

(c) 7 234 000 is [ ] than 7 243 000.

(d) 2 312 478 is [ ] than 2 312 487.

3 Compare using > or <.

(a) 5 498 000 [ ] 4 988 000   (b) 3 456 000 [ ] 3 478 000

(c) 4 000 102 [ ] 4 000 099   (d) 1 000 001 [ ] 1 000 010

Comparing and ordering numbers to 10 000 000

Starter

Ruby researched some of the most popular tourist attractions in the world for a school project.

She placed the approximate number of visitors to each attraction in a table.

Attraction	Visitors
Colosseum (Italy)	7 618 000
Louvre (France)	9 600 000
Vatican (Vatican City)	6 800 000
Statue of Liberty (United States)	4 240 000
Eiffel Tower (France)	6 100 000
Sagrada Familia (Spain)	4 700 000

What can Ruby say about this information?

Example

Ruby can compare the number of visitors to find the most popular tourist attraction in her table.

The first and second most popular attractions can be found by looking at the millions place.

Louvre (France)	9 600 000
Colosseum (Italy)	7 618 000

Both these attractions have a greater number of millions than the other numbers.

The Vatican and the Eiffel Tower had at least 6 million visitors. Look at the hundred-thousands place to see which attraction had more visitors.

| Vatican (Vatican City) | 6 800 000 |
| Eiffel Tower (France) | 6 100 000 |

The Vatican had more visitors than the Eiffel Tower.

6 800 000 > 6 100 000

The two smallest numbers both have 4 millions.

The hundred-thousands place will show us which is the greater number.

| Statue of Liberty (United States) | 4 240 000 |
| Sagrada Familia (Spain) | 4 700 000 |

The Statue of Liberty had fewer visitors than the Sagrada Familia.

4 240 000 < 4 700 000

Now that we have compared the numbers of visitors, we can order them from smallest to greatest.

4 240 000, 4 700 000, 6 100 000, 6 800 000, 7 618 000, 9 600 000

smallest   ⟶   greatest

The Louvre had more visitors than any of the other tourist attractions.

The Statue of Liberty had the smallest number of visitors.

Practice

The table shows the population of some US states.

US state	Population
Maryland	6 177 224
Missouri	6 154 913
Colorado	5 773 714
Minnesota	5 706 494
Alabama	5 024 279
Massachusetts	7 029 917

Look at the digit in each place to help you compare.

1   (a)   The state with the greatest population is [   ] .

(b)   Minnesota has a greater population than [   ] .

(c)   The state with the smallest population is [   ] .

(d)   Maryland has a smaller population than [   ] .

2   Put the populations in order from smallest to greatest.

[   ] , [   ] , [   ] , [   ] , [   ] , [   ]

3   Compare using >, < or =.

(a)   3 400 000 [   ] 4 100 000   (b)   910 000 [   ] 1 200 000

(c)   2 205 180 [   ] 2 201 000   (d)   8 763 413 [   ] 8 760 998

4   Use the following numbers to fill in the blanks.

6 520 141		6 534 999		523 518

	5 653 141		623 499		6 535 421

[   ] > [   ]

[   ] < [   ]

[   ] > [   ]

10, 100 and 1000 times greater and smaller

Starter

The distance between the Earth and the Moon is approximately 400 000 km. The distance around the circumference of the Earth is approximately 40 000 km. The distance between the United Kingdom and Egypt is approximately 4000 km. How can we compare these distances?

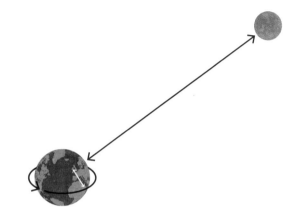

Example

Show the first two distances in a place-value chart.

millions	hundred thousands	ten thousands	thousands	hundreds	tens	ones
	4	0	0	0	0	0
		4	0	0	0	0

The value of 4 in 400 000 is 10 times greater than the value of 4 in 40 000.

The value of 4 in 40 000 is 10 times smaller than the value of 4 in 400 000.

millions	hundred thousands	ten thousands	thousands	hundreds	tens	ones
		4	0	0	0	0
			4	0	0	0

The value of 4 in 40 000 is 10 times greater than the value of 4 in 4000.

The value of 4 in 4000 is 10 times smaller than the value of 4 in 40 000.

When the place of a digit changes, so does its value.

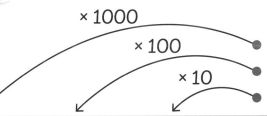

× 1000
× 100
× 10

millions	hundred thousands	ten thousands	thousands	hundreds	tens	ones
4	0	0	0	0	0	0
	4	0	0	0	0	0
		4	0	0	0	0
			4	0	0	0

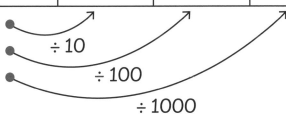

÷ 10
÷ 100
÷ 1000

We can see that 4 000 000 is 1000 times greater than 4000, 100 times greater than 40 000 and 10 times greater than 400 000.

4000 is 1000 times smaller than 4 000 000, 100 times smaller than 400 000 and 10 times smaller than 40 000.

Practice

Fill in the blanks.

1

millions	hundred thousands	ten thousands	thousands	hundreds	tens	ones

(a) The value of 3 in 4 356 000 is [_____] greater than the value of 3 in 2 534 000.

(b) The value of 6 in 6 125 000 is [_____] greater than the value of 6 in 3 756 000.

(c) The value of 7 in 3 997 000 is [_____] smaller than the value of 7 in 7 443 000.

(d) The value of 9 in 4 221 900 is [_____] smaller than the value of 9 in 9 030 000.

2 (a) [_____] is 100 times greater than 1000.

(b) 800 000 is 1000 times greater than [_____].

(c) 7 200 000 is [_____] greater than 7200.

(d) 4980 is 100 times smaller than [_____].

3 There are approximately 5000 people at a half marathon in Manchester, UK.
There are 10 times as many people at a marathon in New York, US.
How many people are at the marathon in New York?

[_____]

There are [_____] people at the marathon in New York.

4 The distance between Ruby's house and her grandmother's house is 18 km.
The approximate distance between London, United Kingdom, and Auckland, New Zealand, is 1000 times greater than the distance between Ruby's house and her grandmother's house.
What is the approximate distance between London and Auckland?

[_____]

The approximate distance between London and Auckland is
[_____] km.

Locating numbers on a number line

Starter

At a school fair, a prize was given to the person who could most accurately mark 478 ml on a 1-l jug of water.
Where would you mark 478 ml on the jug?

Example

I know that 500 ml is half of 1 l so 500 ml is halfway.

I also know that there are 250 ml between the first marking and halfway. I can imagine that section divided into 5 equal steps.

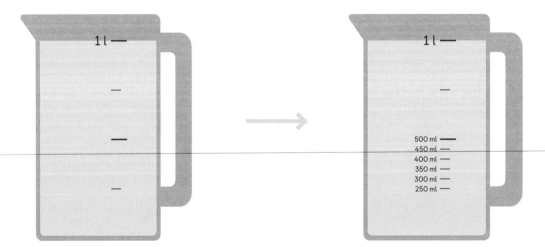

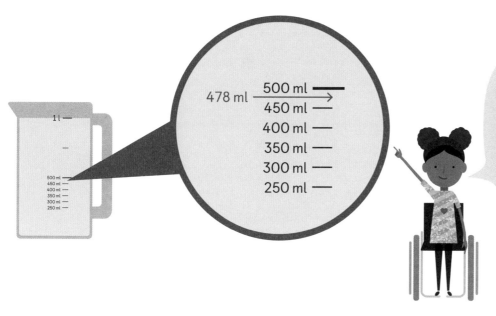

Estimate the position of the following numbers on a number line.

19 500

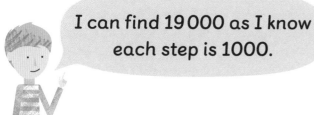

I can find 19 000 as I know each step is 1000.

I know that 19 500 is exactly halfway between 19 000 and 20 000.

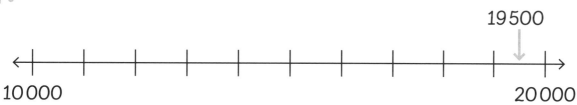

253 700

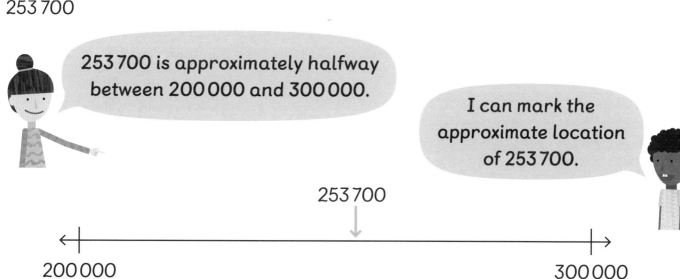

253 700 is approximately halfway between 200 000 and 300 000.

I can mark the approximate location of 253 700.

321 456

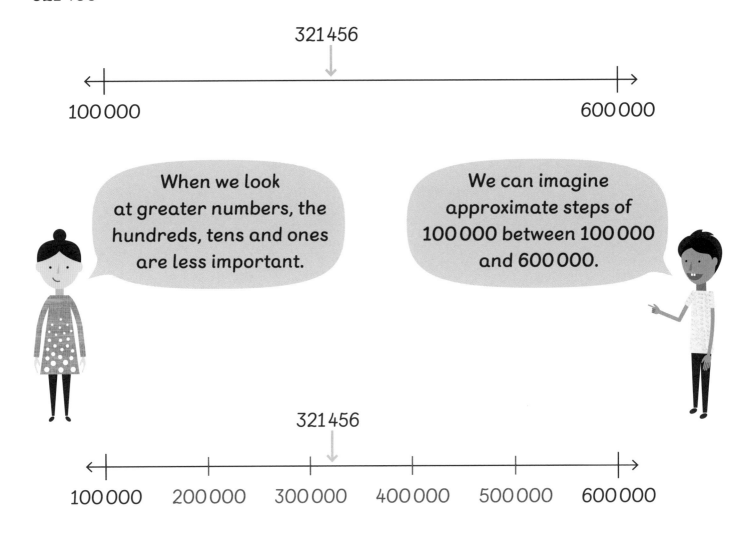

When we look at greater numbers, the hundreds, tens and ones are less important.

We can imagine approximate steps of 100 000 between 100 000 and 600 000.

Practice

1 Place the following numbers on the number line.

(a) 60 000   45 000   22 000

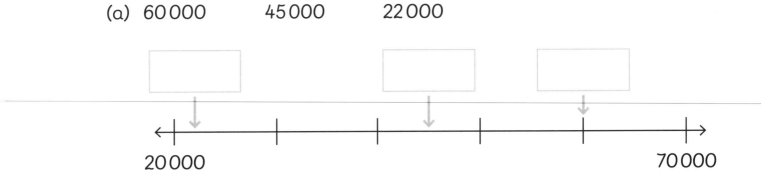

(b) 450 000   625 000   240 000

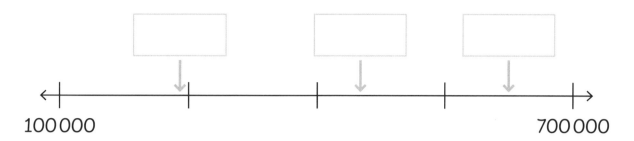

(c) 360 109   460 109   317 463

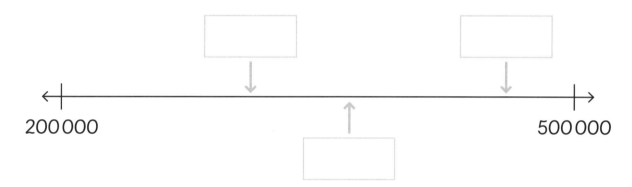

2 Estimate the missing numbers and fill in the blanks.

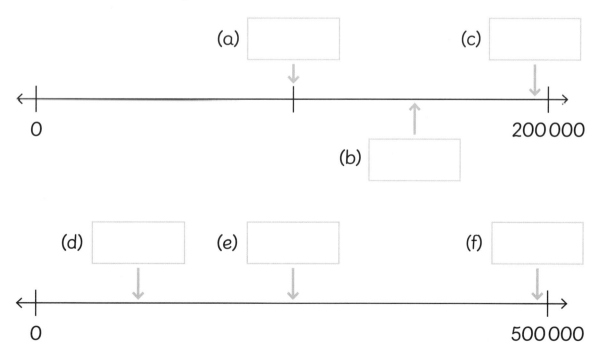

Rounding numbers (part 1)

Starter

The table shows the number of people that changed trains at each station during one year.

Train station	Number of people
London Waterloo	6 310 000
London Victoria	5 756 000
London Liverpool Street	4 351 000
Sheffield	1 050 000
Birmingham New Street	6 994 000

Approximately how many people changed trains at each station?

Example

Round 6 310 000 to the nearest million.

London Waterloo: 6 310 000

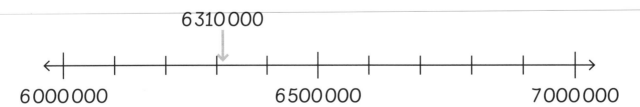

6 310 000 is closer to 6 000 000 than to 7 000 000.

If the hundred-thousands place has a value of 0, 1, 2, 3 or 4, the number in the millions place stays the same when rounding to the nearest million.

6 310 000 is rounded to 6 000 000 when rounding to the nearest million.

6 310 000 is approximately 6 000 000.

6 310 000 ≈ 6 000 000 (to the nearest 1 000 000)

London Victoria: 5 756 000

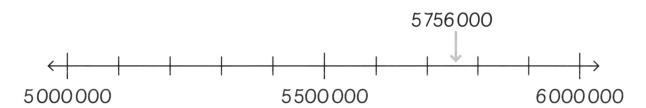

5 756 000

5 000 000   5 500 000   6 000 000

If the hundred-thousands place has a value of 5, 6, 7, 8 or 9, the number in the millions place increases when rounding to the nearest million.

5 756 000 is closer to 6 000 000 than to 5 000 000.

5 756 000 is rounded to 6 000 000 when rounding to the nearest million.

5 756 000 is approximately 6 000 000.

5 756 000 ≈ 6 000 000 (to the nearest 1 000 000)

Sheffield: 1 050 000

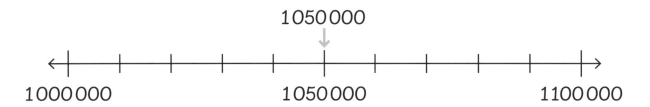

1 050 000 is rounded to 1 100 000 when rounding to the nearest hundred thousand.

1 050 000 is approximately 1 100 000.

1 050 000 ≈ 1 100 000 (to the nearest 100 000)

Practice

Round to the nearest 1 000 000.

1 (a) London Liverpool Street: 4 351 000

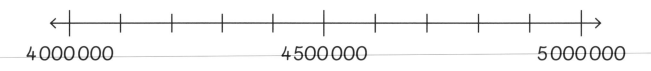

4 351 000 ≈ ⬚ (to the nearest 1 000 000)

(b) Birmingham New Street: 6 994 000

6 994 000 ≈ [   ] (to the nearest 1 000 000)

2 Fill in the blanks to complete the sentences.

(a) 3 780 000 ≈ [   ] (to the nearest 1 000 000)

(b) 6 212 000 ≈ [   ] (to the nearest 1 000 000)

(c) 8 099 000 ≈ [   ] (to the nearest 1 000 000)

3 Ravi rounds two numbers to the nearest 1 000 000 and then adds them together to get a total of 7 000 000.

(a) If both numbers were rounded up and one number was less than 3 000 000 to start with, what are the greatest numbers each could have been before being rounded?

[   ]   [   ]

(b) If both numbers were rounded down and one number was greater than 5 000 000 to start with, what are the smallest numbers each could have been before being rounded?

[   ]   [   ]

Rounding numbers (part 2)

Starter

Mauritius is an island in the Indian Ocean. In 2020, the population of Mauritius was 1 265 740. How can we describe the population of Mauritius?

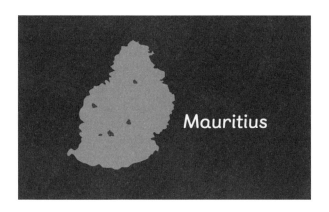

Mauritius

Example

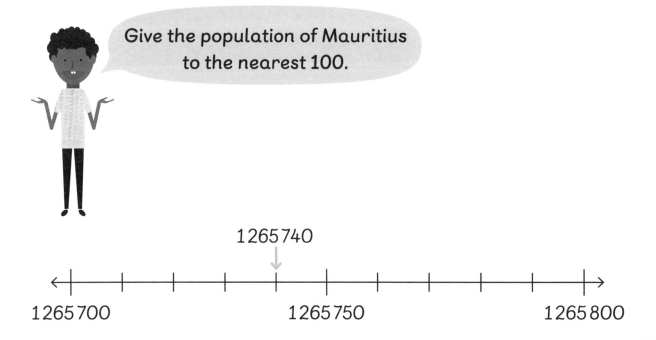

Give the population of Mauritius to the nearest 100.

1 265 740

1 265 700   1 265 750   1 265 800

1 265 740 is 1 265 700 when rounded to the nearest hundred.

1 265 740 is approximately 1 265 700.

1 265 740 ≈ 1 265 700 (to the nearest 100)

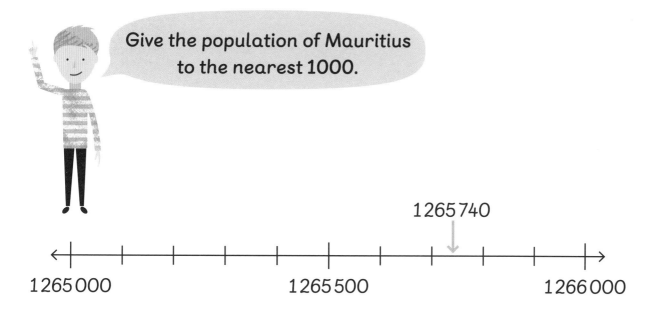

Give the population of Mauritius to the nearest 1000.

1265740

1265000 1265500 1266000

1265740 is 1266000 when rounded to the nearest thousand.

1265740 is approximately 1266000.

1265740 ≈ 1266000 (to the nearest 1000)

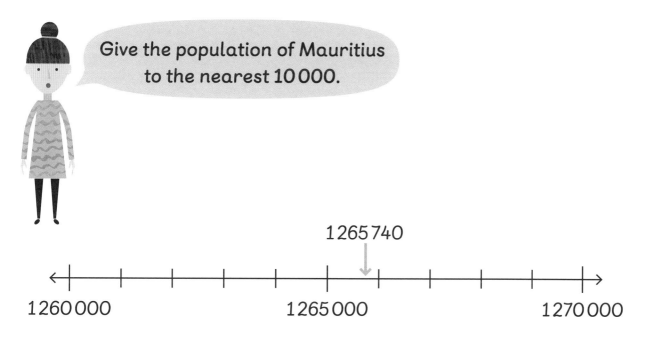

Give the population of Mauritius to the nearest 10000.

1265740

1260000 1265000 1270000

1265740 is 1270000 when rounded to the nearest ten thousand.

1265740 is approximately 1270000.

1265740 ≈ 1270000 (to the nearest 10000)

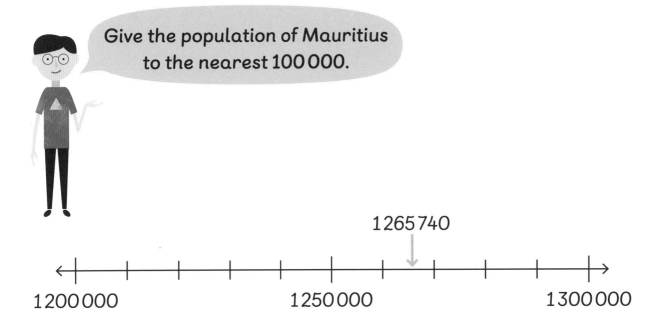

Give the population of Mauritius to the nearest 100 000.

1265 740 is 1 300 000 when rounded to the nearest hundred thousand.

1265 740 is approximately 1 300 000.

1265 740 ≈ 1 300 000 (to the nearest 100 000)

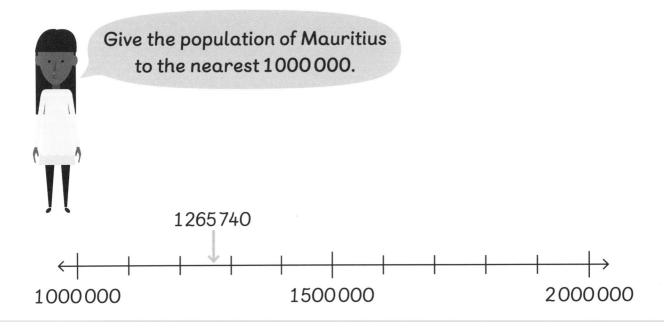

Give the population of Mauritius to the nearest 1 000 000.

1265 740 is 1 000 000 when rounded to the nearest million.

1265 740 is approximately 1 000 000.

1265 740 ≈ 1 000 000 (to the nearest 1 000 000)

1 The population of Botswana in 2020 was 2 351 630.

(a) 2 351 630 is [   ] when rounded to the nearest hundred.

2 351 630 ≈ [   ] (to the nearest 100)

(b) 2 351 630 is [   ] when rounded to the nearest thousand.

2 351 630 ≈ [   ] (to the nearest 1000)

(c) 2 351 630 is [   ] when rounded to the nearest

ten thousand.

2 351 630 ≈ [   ] (to the nearest 10 000)

(d) 2 351 630 is [   ] when rounded to the nearest

hundred thousand.

2 351 630 ≈ [   ] (to the nearest 100 000)

(e) 2 351 630 is [   ] when rounded to the nearest million.

2 351 630 ≈ [   ] (to the nearest 1 000 000)

2 Fill in the blanks.

(a) 3 472 312 is 3 500 000 when rounded to the nearest [   ].

(b) 7 112 498 is 7 112 500 when rounded to the nearest [   ].

(c) 5 615 492 is 5 620 000 when rounded to the nearest [   ].

Negative numbers (part 1)

Starter

Emma needed to remember where her family parked the car in the car park.
She saw this sign.
What does the sign tell us about where they parked?

Example

We read −2 as negative 2.
We can show −2 on a number line.

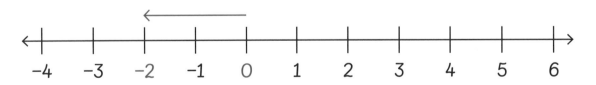

−4 −3 −2 −1 0 1 2 3 4 5 6

Negative numbers are less than zero.

−2 is 2 less than 0.

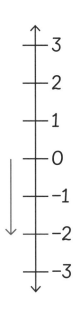

The car park has 7 floors.
The ground floor is marked 0.

Level −2 is 2 floors below
the ground floor or level 0.

Practice

1 Fill in the blanks.

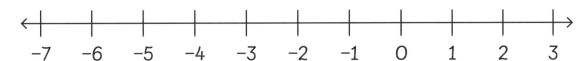

-7 -6 -5 -4 -3 -2 -1 0 1 2 3

(a) [ ] is 1 less than 0.

(b) [ ] is 3 less than 0.

(c) [ ] is 5 less than 0.

(d) −4 is [ ] less than 0.

(e) −6 is [ ] less than 0.

(f) −7 is [ ] less than 0.

Negative numbers (part 2)

Starter

Miss Fathima asked her class to look at the average day and night temperatures in January of different cities around the world.
Which city had the greatest difference in temperature between day and night?

City		Day (°C)	Night (°C)
	Vienna	3	−2
	Toronto	−1	−7
	Prague	3	−1
	Munich	3	−3
	Geneva	5	−1
	Denver	9	−7

Example

 Vienna

We read °C as degrees Celsius. This is a unit of measurement used to measure temperature.

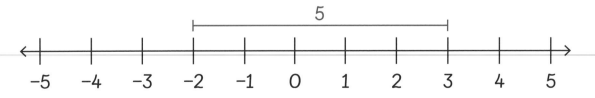

The difference between 3 °C and −2 °C is 5 degrees.
The temperature decreased by 5 °C from day to night.

3 is a positive number. It is 3 greater than 0.

3 °C is 3 degrees greater than 0 °C.

 Prague

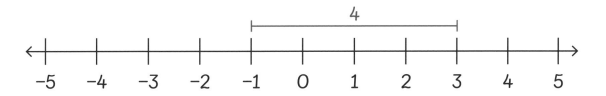

The difference between 3 °C and −1 °C is 4 degrees.
The temperature decreased by 4 °C from day to night.

 Munich

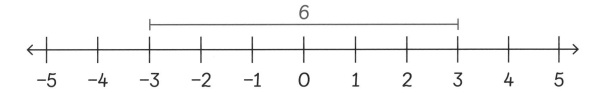

The difference between 3 and −3 is 6.
The temperature decreased by 6 degrees from 3 °C to −3 °C.

 Denver

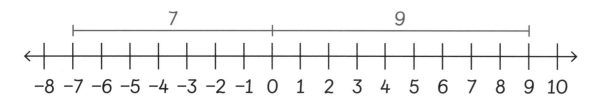

The difference between 9 and −7 is 16.
The temperature decreased by 16 degrees from 9 °C to −7 °C.

Practice

1 Find the difference between the average day and night temperatures of the following cities.

(a) Geneva   Day: 5 °C   Night: −1 °C

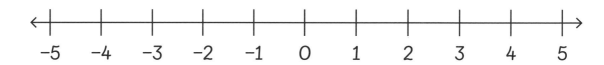

The difference between 5 and −1 is ▢.

(b) Toronto   Day: −1 °C   Night: −7 °C

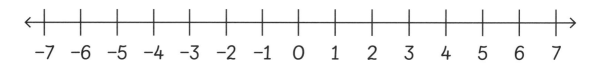

The difference between −1 and −7 is ▢.

2 Fill in the blanks.

````
←—+——+——+——+——+——+——+——+——+——+——+——+——+——+——+——+——+——+——+→
   -9  -8  -7  -6  -5  -4  -3  -2  -1   0   1   2   3   4   5   6   7   8   9
````

(a) The difference between 3 and −4 is ____ .

(b) The difference between 5 and −1 is ____ .

(c) The difference between 8 and −8 is ____ .

(d) The difference between 0 and −9 is ____ .

3 When Ravi woke up the temperature was 4 °C. By lunchtime, the temperature had increased by 5 °C. At 10 p.m. when Ravi went to bed, the temperature was 10 °C less than the temperature at lunchtime.
What was the temperature when Ravi went to bed?

The temperature when Ravi went to bed was ____ °C.

4 The temperature at 7 a.m. in Edmonton, Canada, was −17 °C.
On the same day, the temperature in Darwin, Australia, was 46 °C greater than the temperature in Edmonton.
What was the temperature in Darwin?

The temperature in Darwin was ____ °C.

Adding and subtracting negative numbers

Starter

Charles started with −1.
He then took two more cards as part of a game he was playing with Oak.
Is it possible to add to negative numbers?
Is it possible to subtract from negative numbers?

Example

−1 + 5 = ☐

Add 5 to −1.

Start at −1 and count on 5 using the number line.

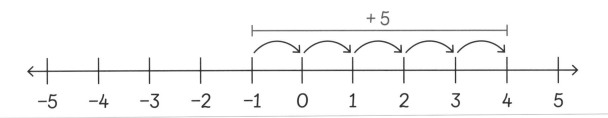

−1 + 5 = 4

-1 $- 5$ $=$ ☐

Subtract 5 from −1 by counting backwards.

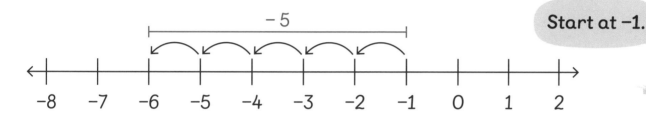

Start at −1.

−1 − 5 = −6

Oak took these cards.

☐ $- 3$ $=$ -2

Start at −2 and add the amount that has been subtracted.

What could ☐ be?

☐ = 1

1 − 3 = −2

Practice

Fill in the blanks.

1
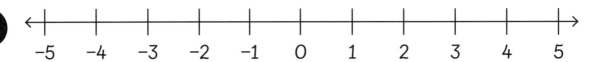

(a) −1 + 3 = ☐

(b) −2 + 4 = ☐

(c) −1 + 6 = ☐

(d) −4 + 6 = ☐

(e) −3 + 3 = ☐

(f) −5 + 10 = ☐

2
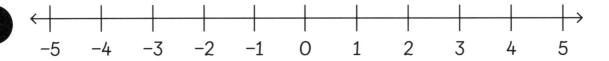

(a) 2 − 3 = ☐

(b) 3 − 5 = ☐

(c) −1 − 2 = ☐

(d) 2 − 6 = ☐

(e) 0 − 5 = ☐

(f) −1 − 1 = ☐

3 (a) −3 + 7 = ☐

(b) −5 + 12 = ☐

(c) −13 + 6 = ☐

(d) 5 − 6 = ☐

(e) 8 − 10 = ☐

(f) −7 − 8 = ☐

4 The temperature in Toronto was 6 °C at 3 p.m.
At 10 p.m. the temperature was 8 °C lower than at 3 p.m.
What was the temperature at 10 p.m.?

The temperature at 10 p.m. was ⬚ °C.

5 Ravi's mum drives into the entrance to the car park at level 1.
She drives down to level 0 and then drives another 3 levels down before parking her car.
Which level has Ravi's mum parked on?

Ravi's mum has parked on level ⬚.

Review and challenge

1 7 421 956

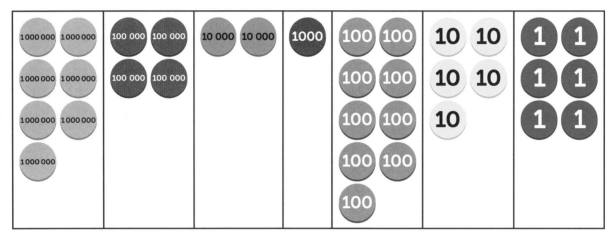

(a) The 7 in 7 421 956 has a value of [   ].

It is in the [   ] place.

(b) The 4 in 7 421 956 has a value of [   ].

It is in the [   ] place.

(c) The 2 in 7 421 956 has a value of [   ].

It is in the [   ] place.

(d) The 1 in 7 421 956 has a value of [   ].

It is in the [   ] place.

(e) The 9 in 7 421 956 has a value of [   ].

It is in the [   ] place.

(f) The 5 in 7 421 956 has a value of [ ].

It is in the [ ] place.

(g) The 6 in 7 421 956 has a value of [ ].

It is in the [ ] place.

2 Compare using >, < or =.

(a) 1000000 100000 100000 100000 **10 10 1** [ ] 1000000 1000000 **1 1 1**

(b) 1000000 1000000 1000000 100000 10000 [ ] 100000 100000 100000 100000 100000 **10 10**

(c) 1000000 100000 **1000 1000 1000** [ ] 1000000 100000 10000

(d) 1000000 1000000 **10 10 1** [ ] 1000000 1000000 **10 10 1**

3 Compare using >, < or =.

(a) 3 459 000 [ ] 3 459 000

(b) 389 250 [ ] 1 450 000

(c) 5 619 300 [ ] 5 624 100

(d) 8 936 218 [ ] 8 936 128

4 Put the numbers in order from smallest to greatest.

435 712   399 876   1 202 396   5 000 827   4 357 120

[ ] , [ ] , [ ] , [ ] , [ ]

smallest   greatest

5 Round the following numbers.

(a) 423 000 ≈ [ ]   (to the nearest 100 000)

(b) 1 856 000 ≈ [ ]   (to the nearest 1 000 000)

(c) 5 678 000 ≈ [ ]   (to the nearest 10 000)

(d) 8 099 216 ≈ [ ]   (to the nearest 1 000 000)

6 Fill in the blanks.

(a) $-1 + 2 =$ [ ]   (b) $-4 + 7 =$ [ ]

(c) $-5 + 5 =$ [ ]   (d) $4 - 5 =$ [ ]

(e) $-3 - 4 =$ [ ]   (f) $-12 - 10 =$ [ ]

7 Multiply.

(a) 5000 × 10 = [   ]

(b) 6000 × 100 = [   ]

(c) 300 × 1000 = [   ]

(d) 4000 × [   ] = 4 000 000

(e) 20 × [   ] = 20 000

(f) [   ] × 1000 = 3 000 000

8 Jacob multiplied a number by 10 and then by 100.
If the product he ended with was 4 000 000, what was the number he started with?

[   ]

Jacob started with the number [   ].

9 Oak wrote the following number using words:

twelve million, twenty-three hundred thousands, fourteen ten thousands, eighty-six hundreds and twenty-one ones

Write the number in numerals.

[   ]

Answers

Page 5   **1 (a)** 5 620 000 **(b)** 2 132 111 **2 (a)** two million, four hundred and fifty-six thousand
(b) six million, one hundred and twenty-five thousand, two hundred and thirty
(c) eight million, nine hundred and twelve thousand, six hundred and fifty-two

Page 7   **1 (a)** 4 532 128 = 4 000 000 + 500 000 + 30 000 + 2000 + 100 + 20 + 8
(b) 7 659 382 = 7 000 000 + 600 000 + 50 000 + 9000 + 300 + 80 + 2
(c) 2 413 926 = 2 000 000 + 400 000 + 10 000 + 3000 + 900 + 20 + 6
2 (a) 1000 is 1000 times greater than 1. **(b)** 30 000 is 10 times greater than 3000.
(c) 4000 is 100 times smaller than 400 000. **(d)** 8000 is 1000 times smaller
than 8 000 000.

Page 11   **1 (a)** 3 200 000 < 4 200 000 **(b)** 3 200 000 < 4 110 000 **(c)** 2 130 000 > 1 500 000
(d) 1 130 000 > 1 112 000 **2 (a)** 6 800 000 is greater than 5 800 000.
(b) 4 030 000 is greater than 4 003 000. **(c)** 7 234 000 is less than 7 243 000.
(d) 2 312 478 is less than 2 312 487. **3 (a)** 5 498 000 > 4 988 000
(b) 3 456 000 < 3 478 000 **(c)** 4 000 102 > 4 000 099 **(d)** 1 000 001 < 1 000 010

Page 15   **1 (a)** The state with the greatest population is Massachusetts. **(b)** Minnesota has
a greater population than Alabama. **(c)** The state with the smallest population is
Alabama. **(d)** Maryland has a smaller population than Massachusetts. **2** Alabama,
Minnesota, Colorado, Missouri, Maryland, Massachusetts **3 (a)** 3 400 000 < 4 100 000
(b) 910 000 < 1 200 000 **(c)** 2 205 180 > 2 201 000 **(d)** 8 763 413 > 8 760 998 **4** Answers
will vary. For example: 6 535 421 > 6 534 999, 5 653 141 < 6 520 141, 623 499 > 523 518

Page 18   **1 (a)** The value of 3 in 4 356 000 is 10 times greater than the value of 3 in 2 534 000.
(b) The value of 6 in 6 125 000 is 1000 times greater than the value of 6 in 3 756 000.
(c) The value of 7 in 3 997 000 is 1000 times smaller than the value of 7 in 7 443 000.
(d) The value of 9 in 4 221 900 is 10 000 times smaller than the value of 9 in 9 030 000.

Page 19   **2 (a)** 100 000 is 100 times greater than 1000. **(b)** 800 000 is 1000 times greater
than 800. **(c)** 7 200 000 is 1000 times greater than 7200. **(d)** 4980 is 100 times
smaller than 498 000. **3** There are 50 000 people at the marathon in New York.
4 The approximate distance between London and Auckland is 18 000 km.

Page 22   **1 (a)**

Page 23   **(b)**

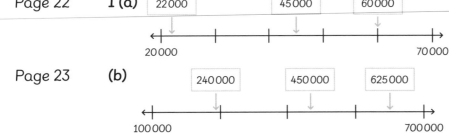

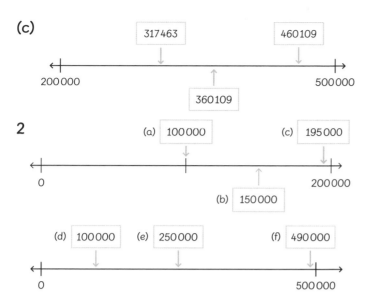

(c)

317463   460109

200000   500000

360109

2

(a) 100000   (c) 195000

0   200000

(b) 150000

(d) 100000   (e) 250000   (f) 490000

0   500000

Page 26   **1 (a)** 4 351 000 ≈ 4 000 000 (to the nearest 1 000 000)

Page 27   **(b)** 6 994 000 ≈ 7 000 000 (to the nearest 1 000 000) **2 (a)** 3 780 000 ≈ 4 000 000 (to the nearest 1 000 000) **(b)** 6 212 000 ≈ 6 000 000 (to the nearest 1 000 000) **(c)** 8 099 000 ≈ 8 000 000 (to the nearest 1 000 000) **3 (a)** 2 999 999, 3 999 999 **(b)** 5 000 001, 2 000 001

Page 31   **1 (a)** 2 351 630 is 2 351 600 when rounded to the nearest hundred. 2 351 630 ≈ 2 351 600 (to the nearest 100) **(b)** 2 351 630 is 2 352 000 when rounded to the nearest thousand. 2 351 630 ≈ 2 352 000 (to the nearest 1000) **(c)** 2 351 630 is 2 350 000 when rounded to the nearest ten thousand. 2 351 630 ≈ 2 350 000 (to the nearest 10 000) **(d)** 2 351 630 is 2 400 000 when rounded to the nearest hundred thousand. 2 351 630 ≈ 2 400 000 (to the nearest 100 000) **(e)** 2 351 630 is 2 000 000 when rounded to the nearest million. 2 351 630 ≈ 2 000 000 (to the nearest 1 000 000) **2 (a)** 3 472 312 is 3 500 000 when rounded to the nearest hundred thousand. **(b)** 7 112 498 is 7 112 500 when rounded to the nearest hundred. **(c)** 5 615 492 is 5 620 000 when rounded to the nearest ten thousand.

Page 33   **1 (a)** −1 is 1 less than 0. **(b)** −3 is 3 less than 0. **(c)** −5 is 5 less than 0. **(d)** −4 is 4 less than 0. **(e)** −6 is 6 less than 0. **(f)** −7 is 7 less than 0.

Page 36   **1 (a)** The difference between 5 and −1 is 6. **(b)** The difference between −1 and −7 is 6.

Page 37   **2 (a)** The difference between 3 and −4 is 7. **(b)** The difference between 5 and −1 is 6. **(c)** The difference between 8 and −8 is 16. **(d)** The difference between 0 and −9 is 9. **3** The temperature when Ravi went to bed was −1 °C. **4** The temperature in Darwin was 29 °C.

Page 40   **1 (a)** −1 + 3 = 2 **(b)** −2 + 4 = 2 **(c)** −1 + 6 = 5 **(d)** −4 + 6 = 2 **(e)** −3 + 3 = 0 **(f)** −5 + 10 = 5 **2 (a)** 2 − 3 = −1 **(b)** 3 − 5 = −2 **(c)** −1 − 2 = −3 **(d)** 2 − 6 = −4 **(e)** 0 − 5 = −5 **(f)** −1 − 1 = −2 **3 (a)** −3 + 7 = 4 **(b)** −5 + 12 = 7 **(c)** −13 + 6 = −7 **(d)** 5 − 6 = −1 **(e)** 8 − 10 = −2 **(f)** −7 − 8 = −15

Answers continued

Page 41   **4** The temperature at 10 p.m. was −2 °C.   **5** Ravi's mum has parked on level −3.

Page 42   **1 (a)** The 7 in 7 421 956 has a value of 7 000 000. It is in the millions place.
(b) The 4 in 7 421 956 has a value of 400 000. It is in the hundred-thousands place.
(c) The 2 in 7 421 956 has a value of 20 000. It is in the ten-thousands place.
(d) The 1 in 7 421 956 has a value of 1000. It is in the thousands place.
(e) The 9 in 7 421 956 has a value of 900. It is in the hundreds place.

Page 43   **(f)** The 5 in 7 421 956 has a value of 50. It is in the tens place.
(g) The 6 in 7 421 956 has a value of 6. It is in the ones place.
2 (a) 1 300 021 < 2 000 003 **(b)** 3 110 000 > 500 020 **(c)** 1 103 000 < 1 110 000
(d) 2 000 021 = 2 000 021 **3 (a)** 3 459 000 = 3 459 000 **(b)** 389 250 < 1 450 000
(c) 5 619 300 < 5 624 100 **(d)** 8 936 218 > 8 936 128

Page 44   **4** 399 876, 435 712, 1 202 396, 4 357 120, 5 000 827 **5 (a)** 423 000 ≈ 400 000 (to the
nearest 100 000) **(b)** 1 856 000 ≈ 2 000 000 (to the nearest 1 000 000) **(c)** 5 678 000
≈ 5 680 000 (to the nearest 10 000) **(d)** 8 099 216 ≈ 8 000 000 (to the nearest
1 000 000) **6 (a)** −1 + 2 = 1 **(b)** −4 + 7 = 3 **(c)** −5 + 5 = 0 **(d)** 4 − 5 = −1 **(e)** −3 − 4 = −7
(f) −12 − 10 = −22

Page 45   **7 (a)** 5000 × 10 = 50 000 **(b)** 6000 × 100 = 600 000 **(c)** 300 × 1000 = 300 000
(d) 4000 × 1000 = 4 000 000 **(e)** 20 × 1000 = 20 000 **(f)** 3000 × 1000 = 3 000 000
8 Jacob started with the number 4000.
9 12 000 000 + 2 300 000 + 140 000 + 8600 + 21 = 14 448 621